RODGERS and HAMMERSTEIN

present

A Musical Play

The King and I ™

Music by

RICHARD RODGERS

Book and Lyrics by

OSCAR HAMMERSTEIN II

Based on the Novel "Anna and the King of Siam"
by
MARGARET LANDON

Directed by JOHN VAN DRUTEN

Settings and lighting by JO MIELZINER

Costumes designed by IRENE SHARAFF

Choreography by JEROME ROBBINS

Orchestrations by ROBERT RUSSELL BENNETT

Musical Director FREDERICK DVONCH

VOCAL SCORE
(Edited by DR. ALBERT SIRMAY)

Vocal Selections also available (HL00312227)

First performance at the St. James Theatre, New York
March 29, 1951

THE KING AND I

Cast of Characters

CAPTAIN ORTON............................Charles Francis

LOUIS LEONOWENS..........................Sandy Kennedy

ANNA LEONOWENS.........................Gertrude Lawrence

THE INTERPRETER..........................Leonard Graves

THE KRALAHOME...........................John Juliano

THE KING................................Yul Brynner

PHRA ALACK.............................Len Mence

TUPTIM.................................Doretta Morrow

LADY THIANG............................Dorothy Sarnoff

PRINCE CHULALONGKORN....................Johnny Stewart

PRINCESS YING YAOWALAK...................Baayork Lee

LUN THA................................Larry Douglas

SIR EDWARD RAMSAY.......................Robin Craven

PRINCESSES AND PRINCES . . . Crisanta Cornejo, Andrea Del Rosario, Marcia James, Barbara Luna, Nora Baez, Corrine St. Denis, Bunny Warner, Rodolfo Cornejo, Robert Cortazal, Thomas Griffin, Alfonso Maribo, James Maribo, Orlando Rodiguez

THE ROYAL DANCERS . . . Jamie Bauer, Lee Becker, Mary Burr, Gemze DeLappe. Shellie Farrell, Marilyn Gennaro, Evelyn Giles, Ina Kurland, Nancy Lynch, Michiko, Helen Murielle, Prue Ward, Dusty Worrall and Yuriko

WIVES . . . Stephanie Augustine, Marcia James, Ruth Korda, Suzanne Lake, Gloria Marlowe, Carolyn Maye, Helen Merritt, Phyllis Wilcox

AMAZONS . . . Geraldine Hamburg, Maribel Hammer, Norma Larkin, Miriam Lawrence

PRIESTS . . . Duane Camp, Joseph Caruso, Leonard Graves, Jack Matthew, Ed Preston

SLAVES . . . Doria Avila, Raul Celada, Beau Cunningham, Tommy Gomez

The Play is Divided into Two Acts.
The Action Passes in and Around the King's Palace, Bangkok, Siam.
Time: Early Eighteen Sixties.

Instrumentation Of Score Is As Follows:

5—VIOLINS [VL]
2—VIOLAS [VA]
2—CELLOS [CL]
1—BASS [B]
2—FLUTES —(1 PIC) [FL]
3—CLARINETS (1 BASS CLAR.) [CLAR]
1—OBOE [OB]

1—BASSOON [BSN]
3—TRUMPETS [TRP]
3—HORNS [HR]
2—TROMBONES [TROM]
1—TUBA [TB]
1—HARP [HP]
1—PERCUSSION [PER]

Seating Plan For Orchestra Of The King And I[TM]

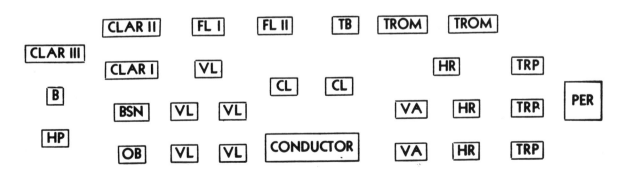

THE KING AND I

Act I

		PAGE
OVERTURE		5
1.	OPENING ACT I (Arrival at Bangkok)	13
2.	I WHISTLE A HAPPY TUNE	15
3.	INCIDENTAL FOR DIALOGUE (Entrance of Kralahome)	22
4.	EXIT: I WHISTLE A HAPPY TUNE	22
5.	VIGNETTES AND DANCE	23
6.	MY LORD AND MASTER	27
7.	INCIDENTAL FOR DIALOGUE	30
8.	HELLO, YOUNG LOVERS	30
9.	ENCORE: HELLO, YOUNG LOVERS	35
10.	THE MARCH OF SIAMESE CHILDREN	38
11.	POSTLUDE TO THE MARCH OF SIAMESE CHILDREN	42
12.	SCENE BEFORE CURTAIN (Priests and Children)	42
13.	A PUZZLEMENT	44
14.	SCHOOL-ROOM SCENE	59
15.	GETTING TO KNOW YOU	61
16.	INCIDENTAL (King)	71
17.	WE KISS IN A SHADOW (Tuptim and Lun Tha)	71
18.	REPRISE: A PUZZLEMENT (Prince and Louis)	78
19.	SHALL I TELL YOU WHAT I THINK OF YOU?	84
20.	SOMETHING WONDERFUL	98
21.	CHANGE OF SCENE (Pantomime)	101
22.	REPRISE: SOMETHING WONDERFUL	101
23.	CHANGE OF SCENE (Postlude to "Something Wonderful")	103
24.	SCENE (Anna and King planning party)	104
25.	FIREWORKS	106
26.	FINALE ACT I	106

Act II

		PAGE
ENTR'ACT		108
27.	OPENING ACT II	113
28.	WESTERN PEOPLE FUNNY	115
29.	EXIT OF WIVES	121
30.	DANCE OF ANNA AND SIR EDWARD	122
31.	EXIT OF ANNA, KING AND SIR EDWARD	124
32.	INCIDENTAL "WE KISS IN A SHADOW"	124
33.	I HAVE DREAMED	126
34.	REPRISE: "HELLO, YOUNG LOVERS"	132
35.	THE SMALL HOUSE OF UNCLE THOMAS (Ballet)	135
36.	POSTLUDE OF BALLET	162
37.	INCIDENTAL (Change of Scene)	164
38.	SONG OF THE KING	165
39.	SHALL WE DANCE?	168
40.	MELOS, MY LORD AND MASTER	178
41.	PROCESSIONAL	179
42.	REPRISE: SOMETHING WONDERFUL (Letter Reading)	184
43.	POLKA DOLOROSO	186
44.	REPRISE: I WHISTLE A HAPPY TUNE	188
45.	FINALE ULTIMO	192
46.	EXIT MUSIC	194

OVERTURE

RICHARD RODGERS

No. 1

Opening Act 1
(Arrival At Bangkok)

Words by
OSCAR HAMMERSTEIN 2nd

Music by
RICHARD RODGERS

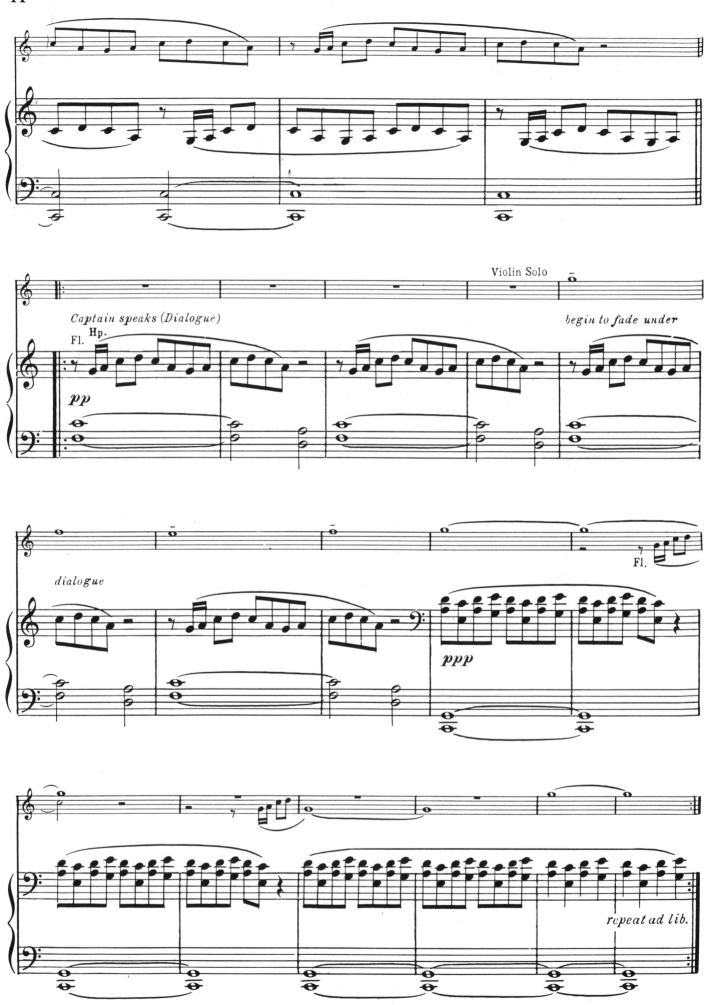

No. 2

I Whistle A Happy Tune

Cue: CAPTAIN ORTON: I think you should know.

shoes I strike a care-less pose And whis-tle a hap-py tune And

no one ev-er knows I'm a-fraid_____ The re-sult of this de-

cep-tion is ver-y strange to— tell For when I fool the

peo-ple I fear I fool my-self as well! I whis-tle a hap-py

tune   And   ev-'ry sin-gle time   The hap-pi-ness in the

tune   con-vin-ces me that I'm not a-fraid.

W.W.

7

Make be-lieve you're brave   And the trick will take you   far.

W.W. & Stgs.

You may be as brave   as you make be-lieve you   are.

11 Make be-lieve you're brave And the trick will take you far. You may be as

p Stgs. & W.W.

brave as you make be-lieve you are. Whistle

Anna notices guards. *Anna (whistles alone) urging*
12 *Louis to whistle too.* *(Louis joins*

Stgs.

in whistling)

pp

No. 3
Incidental For Dialogue
(Entrance of Kralahome)

INTERPRETER: Good evening, Sir Welcome to Siam!
LOUIS: He called you Sir!
ANNA: Hush, dear, hush!

INTERPRETER: Sir, are you lady who will be school mistress of royal children?
ANNA: Yes.
INTERPRETER: Have you friends in Bangkok?
ANNA: I know no one in Bangkok at all.

INTERPRETER: (to Anna) Are you married, sir?
ANNA: I am a widow.
INTERPRETER: What manner of man —— your deceased husband?
ANNA: My husband was an officer of Her Majesty's Army in —— Tell your master his business with me is in my capacity of schoolteacher to the royal children. He has no right to pry into my personal affairs.

No. 4
Exit: I Whistle A Happy Tune

Cue: Goodbye Capt. Orton.

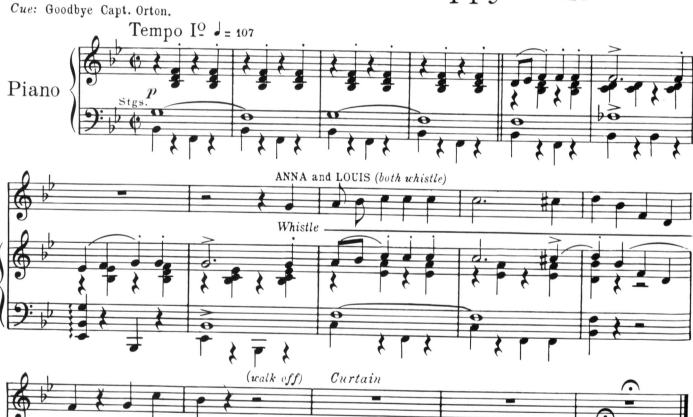

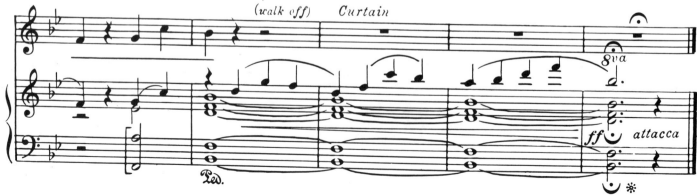

Vignettes And Dance

No. 5

Piano

* *In the New York production the music started here.*

No. 6

My Lord And Master

Cue: KRALAHOME: He is pleased with you. He likes you.

Some-thing young, soft and slim, Paint-ed cheek, tap-'ring limb,

Smil-ing lips all for him. Eyes that shine just for him, So he thinks_

_ just for him. _ Though the man may be _

_ My Lord and Mas - ter _ Though he may stud-y me _

as hard as he can, _____ The smile be-neath my smile _____

W.W. & Br.

—He'll nev-er see _____ He'll nev-er know I love _____ an-oth-er

cresc.

man _____ He'll nev-er know _____ I love an-

Tutti *f*

rit

ff a tempo

molto espressivo

oth - - er man. _____

ed allargando

a tempo
cresc.

ff

Incidental For Dialogue

Cue: *(After King exits)* THIANG: They think you wear big skirt like that because you shaped like that

ANNA: Well, I'm not. *(She lifts her hoopskirt)*

(Wives' pantomime)

After dialogue.

Cue: ANNA: Do you all think women are more lowly than men?

(Thiang translates to wives)

(Wives shake heads)

After dialogue.

THIANG: Tom! (Tom!) *(translates to wives)*

Cue: ANNA: I was very much in love with my late husband, Tom.

Cello

No. 8   Hello, Young Lovers

Cue: ANNA: And she's on their side, even if she's ..... a schoolteacher.

No. 9 Encore: Hello, Young Lovers

After applause.

I've been in love like you, _____ I know how it feels to have wings on your heels And to fly down a street in a trance. _____ You fly down a street on the chance that you'll meet, And you meet_ not real-ly by chance. _____ Don't

No. 10 The March Of Siamese Children

After applause three gongs.
Cue: **KING**: The Royal Princes and Princesses!

Postlude to The March Of Siamese Children

No. 11

Cue: (Anna removes hat)

Scene Before Curtain

No. 12

(Priests And Children)

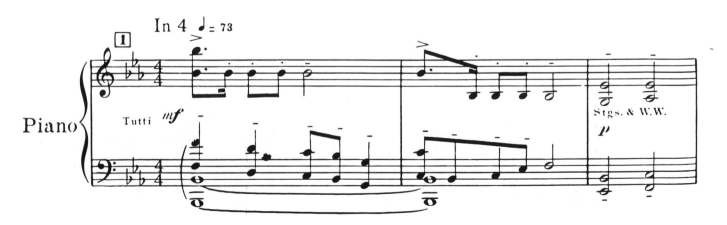

CHILDREN

Be it ev - er so hum - ble, There's

PRIESTS

Oh   Oh

2 *Fade on the dialogue of King and Prince.*

no____ place like home. A charm from the skies seems to hal - low us

Oh

there, Which seek through the world, Is ne'er met___ with else-where.

Oh

A Puzzlement

Cue: **KING:** I do not know. I am not sure.

tell the boy, As far as he is a - ble, _____ To re -

spect his wives and love his con - cu - bines? Shall I

tell him ev - 'ry - one is like the oth - er, _____ And the

bet - ter one of two is real - ly neith - er? _____ If I

tell him this I think he won't be - lieve it,_____ And I

near-ly think I don't be-lieve it eith-er! _____ When my

fa - ther was a king He was a king who knew ex - act - ly what he

knew,_____ And his

bet - ter to be right? Or am I right when I be -

lieve I may be

wrong? _____ Shall I

9 Meno mosso

join with oth - er na - tions in al - li - ance? _____ If al -

life. As a lead-er of my king-dom I must go forth.___ Be

fa-ther to my chil-dren, And hus-band to each wife, Et-

cet-er-a, et-cet-er-a, and so forth.___ If my

Lord in heav-en, Bud-dha, show the way, Ev-'ry

ANNA *(Interrupting)*

Spread out, children.

(Children move downstage)

Now, that last line was 'English words are all we speak.' I didn't quite understand. I want to hear the beginnings and ends of your words. Once again, now, and nice big smiles, because we love our school *(Anna conducts)* One, two, three.

Roy - al Bang - kok A - cad - e - my. If we pay at - ten - tion to our

teach - er And o - bey her ev - 'ry rule, We'll be

grate - ful for those gold - en years, at our dear old school, The

Roy - al Bang - kok A - cad - e - my, Our dear old school. —

cresc. *f*

allargando *rit* *fz*

No. 15

Getting To Know You

Cue: I like you very much indeed.

know you, Get-ting to feel free and eas - y.___ When I am with you, Get-ting to know what to say.___ Hav-en't you no - ticed? Sud-den-ly I'm bright and breez-y ___ be-cause of all the beau-ti-ful and new things I'm learn-ing a-bout you

Schoolroom Dance

WIVES and CHILDREN

Get-ting to know you, Get-ting to feel free and

eas - y ———— When I am with you. Get-ting to know what to

No. 16

Incidental
(King)

Cue: King faces map

Slowly — "So big a world." etc. — No man big enough to be alone. — No man big enough.

Piano Stgs.

Slowly — Cue: King different, King need no one, nobody at all. — I think

Enter Tuptim

No. 17

We Kiss In A Shadow
(Tuptim and Lun Tha)

Cue: TUPTIM: Pretend you wait for her. *(As Lun Tha sits)*

Con sentimento ♩ = 97 — LUN THA: If only we could stop pretending.

Piano Fl. Stgs. Va. Cel.

LUN THA: *(sings)*

We kiss in a sha-dow — We hide from the moon,

No. 18

Reprise: A Puzzlement
(Prince and Louis)

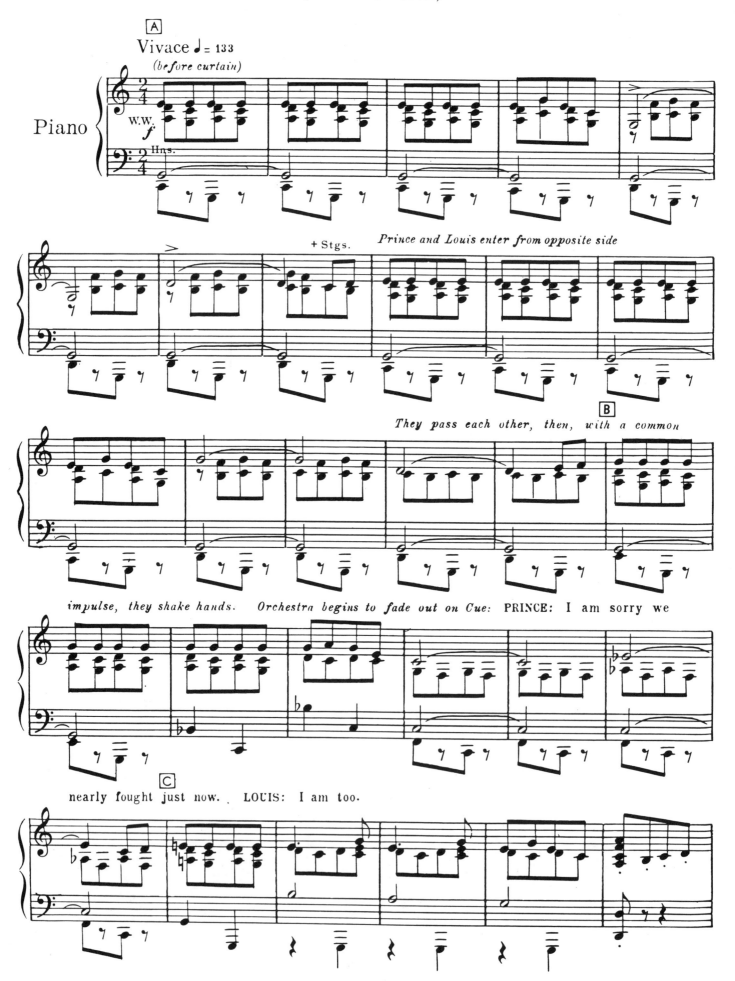

PRINCE: Are you really going away?
LOUIS: Mother plans to leave on the next sailing.
PRINCE: I am not sure my father will allow your mother to go.
LOUIS: I am not sure whether my mother will allow your father not to allow her to go.
PRINCE: Why does not your mother admit that she was wrong?
LOUIS: I don't believe that mother thinks she was wrong.
PRINCE: It begins to look as if people do not know when they are right or wrong - even after they
         have grown up.

Cue: (for music)   LOUIS: I've noticed that too.

PRINCE: J

peo-ple not so bad._____ But no mat-ter what I think, I must go on liv-ing life, And some-day as a lead-er I must go forth,____ Be fath-er to my chil-dren and hus-band to each wife, Et-cet-er-a, et-cet-er-a and so forth.____ If my

No.19 Shall I Tell You What I Think Of You?

Curtain opens disclosing Anna seated on bed.

though you give me less than ser-vant's pay,)_____ I'm a

free and in-de-pend-ent em-ploy-é, em-ploy-

ee. Be-cause I'm a

wo-man, you think like ev-'ry wo-man, I have to be a

(sempre parlando)

kept in coun-ty gaols! In your pur-suit of pleas-ure, You have

mis-tres-ses who treas-ure you. (They have no ken of oth-er men, Be - side whom they can

meas-ure you.) A flock of sheep, and you are the on-ly ram,——— No

won - der you're the won - der of Si - am!

mf

w.w.

teach, _____ They were shy and re-mained out of reach. _____ But late-ly I've thought one or two have been caught By a word I have said or a sen-tence I've read, And I've heard an oc-ca-sion-al quest-ion, _____ That im-

(Sung)

smart   I must leave this place be-fore they break my

heart, _____   I must leave this place be-fore they break my

p   meno   rit

8 Poco mosso

heart. _____

W.W.
Stgs.
pp

(spoken) Goodness! I had no
idea it was so late!

Shall I

Anna adjusts corset

9 Giocoso
(sempre quasi parlando)

tell you what I think of you? You're spoiled! You're a

con-sci-ent-ious work-er But you're spoiled. Giv-ing

cre-dit where it's due, There is much I like in you, But it's

al-so ver-y true that you're spoiled! Ev-'ry-

Something Wonderful

Cue: ANNA: But I simply cannot go to him. I will not.

LADY THIANG: What more can I say to you?

dreams that wont come true, You know that he be - lieves in them, and

that's e -nough for you. You'll al-ways go a-long, De-fend him

when he's wrong, And tell him when he's strong, He is won - der-ful.

He'll al-ways need your love, And so he'll get your love. A man who

needs your love can be won-der-ful. _____

No. 21 Change of Scene
(Pantomine)

Anna and Lady Thiang exit.

No. 22 Reprise: Something Wonderful

LADY THIANG:
But this I think she doesn't know.

(sings)

She'll al-ways go a-long, De-fend him when he's wrong

And tell him when he's strong, He is won-der-ful. He'll al-ways

need her love, And so he'll get her love. A man who

needs your love can be won-der-ful.

rit. *allargando* *ff attacca*

No. 23

Change of Scene
(Postlude to "Something Wonderful")

Poco maestoso

Curtain

Piano

Tutti *f /espr.*
R.H. L.H.
R.H. L.H.
Stgs.
W.W.
H.ns.

(King sees Anna)
Vn.Cl.

cresc. e rit.

fp Stgs. *p più mosso*
W.W.

Va.
f in tempo

Molto meno   ANNA: Your Majesty! Your Majesty!

Stgs.

dim. e rit.

L.H.
p lontano

Scene
(Anna And King Planning Party)

Cue: KING: You mean dress them in dresses.

No. 25

Fireworks

Warning: Above all I must not be disturbed.

Cue: Explosion.

No. 26

Finale Act I

Cue: Bow to him.
Bow! Bow! Bow!
Bow!

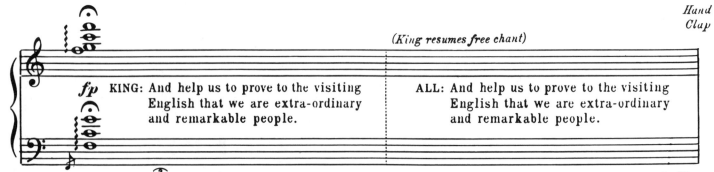

Hand
clap

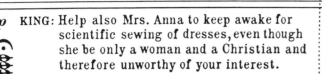

fp KING: Help also Mrs. Anna to keep awake for scientific sewing of dresses, even though she be only a woman and a Christian and therefore unworthy of your interest.

ALL: Help also Mrs. Anna to keep awake for scientific sewing of dresses, even though she be only a woman and a Christian and therefore unworthy of your interest.

Dolce

Va. Cl.
slowly

p KING: And Buddha, I promise you that I shall give this unworthy woman.........

A house of her own | A brick residence | Adjoining the Royal Palace

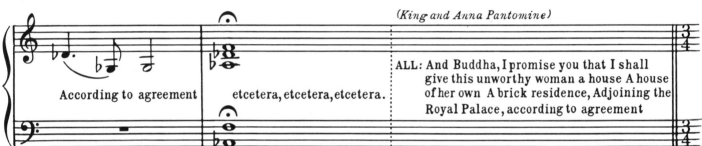

(King and Anna Pantomine)

According to agreement | etcetera, etcetera, etcetera.

ALL: And Buddha, I promise you that I shall give this unworthy woman a house A house of her own A brick residence, Adjoining the Royal Palace, according to agreement

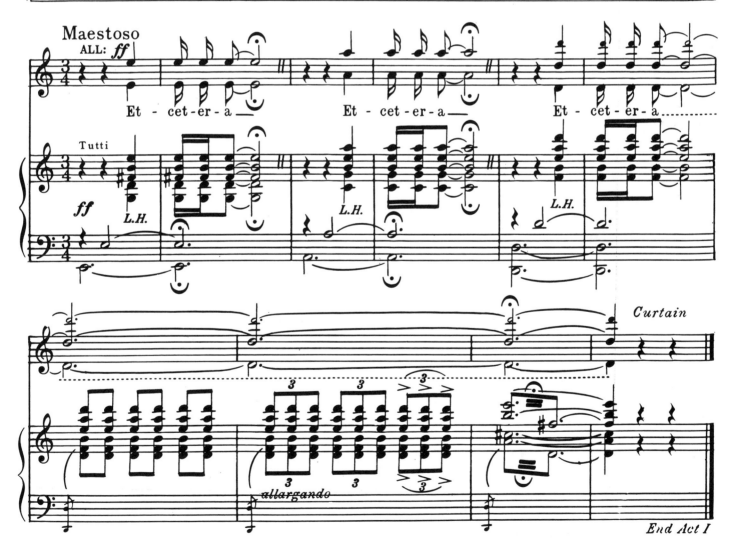

Maestoso
ALL: *ff*

Et - cet-er - a____ Et - cet-er - a____ Et - cet-er - a.............

Tutti
ff
L.H.

L.H.

L.H.

Curtain

allargando

End Act I

Entr' Act

Alla barcarolla

No. 27

Opening Act II

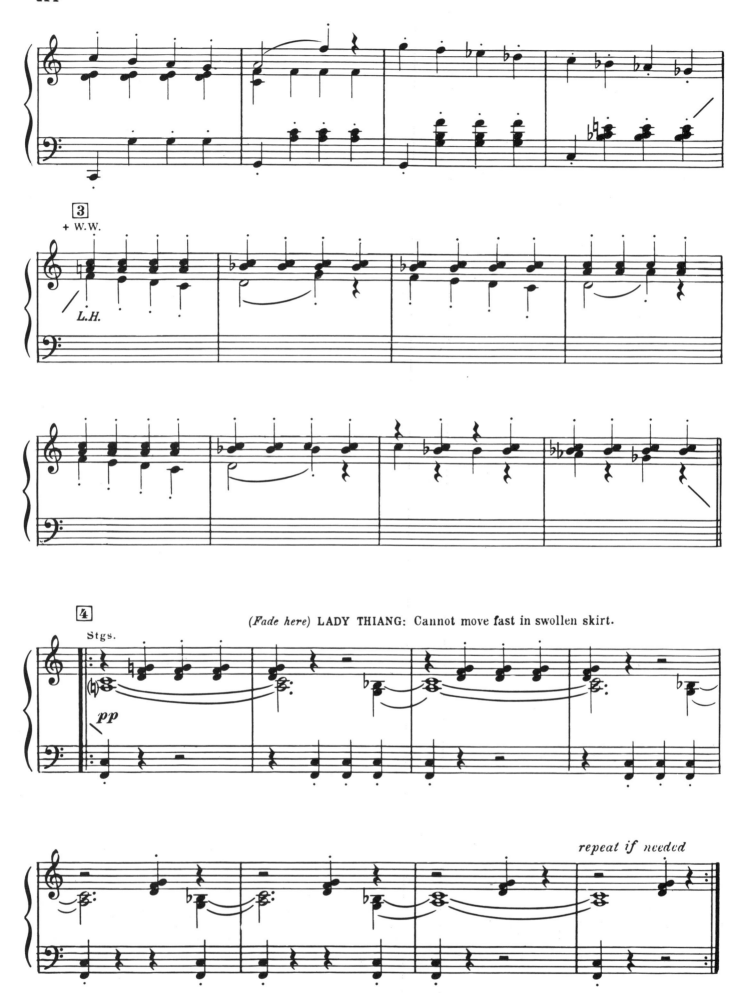

(Fade here) LADY THIANG: Cannot move fast in swollen skirt.

repeat if needed

No. 28 # Western People Funny

Cue: **LADY THIANG:** Whatever Mrs. Anna want us to do is wise and good, but this....

learn to make the same mis-take That they are mak-ing too!

THIANG: Ah

All: They think they civ - il - ize us when - ev - er they ad - vise us. To

Ah

learn to make the same mis-take that they are mak-ing too.

They make quite a few!

ff Tutti

attacca

Exit

(Fade as King enters)

No. 29

Exit Of Wives

A WIFE: Evil eye, evil eye!

No. 30 Dance Of Anna And Sir Edward

Cue: KRALAHOME: Your excellency.

Slow, elegant Valse *(under dialogue)* ♩ = 100

Fade as King says: **Dancing after dinner.**

repeat until Cue:"Dancing after dinner"

No. 31 Exit Of Anna, King And Sir Edward

Cue: KING: Yes, better be going in, Anna.

No. 32 Incidental "We Kiss In A Shadow"

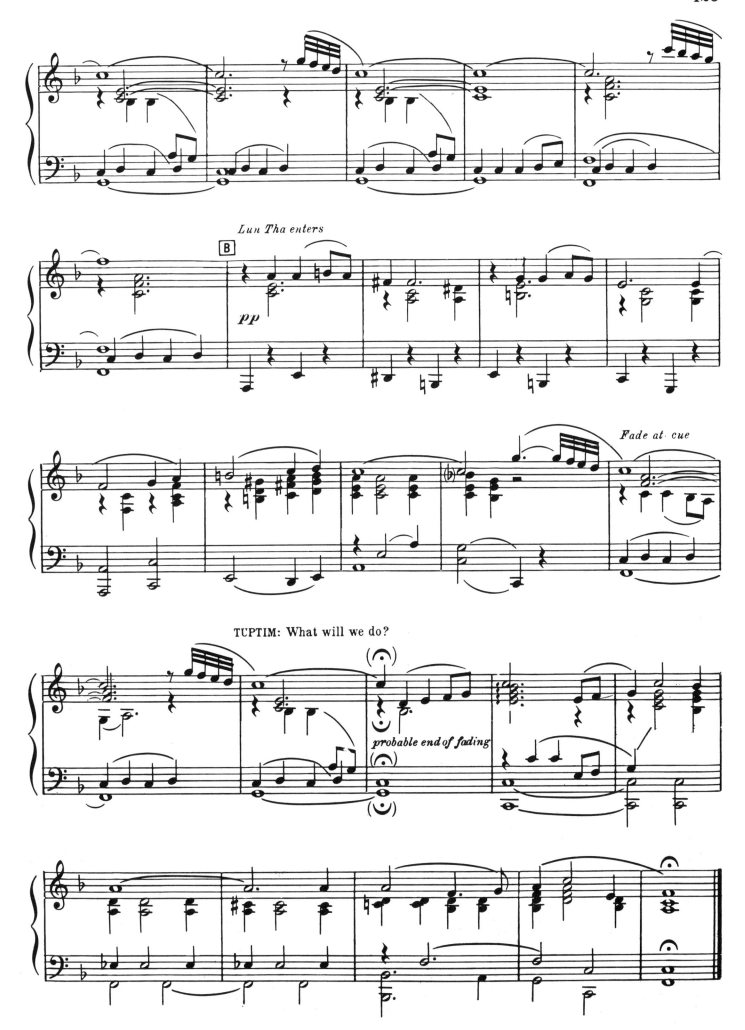

No. 33   # I Have Dreamed

Cue: TUPTIM: I cannot believe it.

so That by now I think I know What it's like to be

loved by you, _____ I will love be-ing loved by

cresc.

f

espr.
Br.
Tutti

rit

Poco piu mosso ♩ = 97

Finish

3

TUPTIM

you. _____ A - lone and a - wake, I've

mf
Stgs.W.W +Hp.

p

molto legato

looked at the stars, The same that smiled on

dreams I've loved you so That by now I think I

TUPTIM

know What it's like to be loved by you,_____

LUN THA

What it's like to be loved_ by ___ you, loved by

cresc.

Tutti *fallargando*

___ I will love be - ing loved by you.

you, I will love be - ing loved by you.

molto rit.

ff

attacca

Reprise: "Hello, Young Lovers"

cry, young lov-ers, what-ev-er you do, Don't cry be-cause I'm a-lone, All of my mem-'ries are hap-py to-night, I've had a love of my own. _____ I've had a love of my own, like yours, I've had a love of my own. _____

Tutti cresc.

f

R.H.

No. 35 The Small House Of Uncle Thomas
(Ballet)

A Siamese musician enters, beating a gong in walking rhythm. He is followed by servant who carries his drum and ratchet. Other servants place benches for a chorus of girls and a stool for the musician on opposite sides of the stage. While gong beating continues, chorus enter, bow to the audience and take their places. Then the narrator, Tuptim, enters and after bowing to the audience, sits down in front of the chorus. (Gong stops)

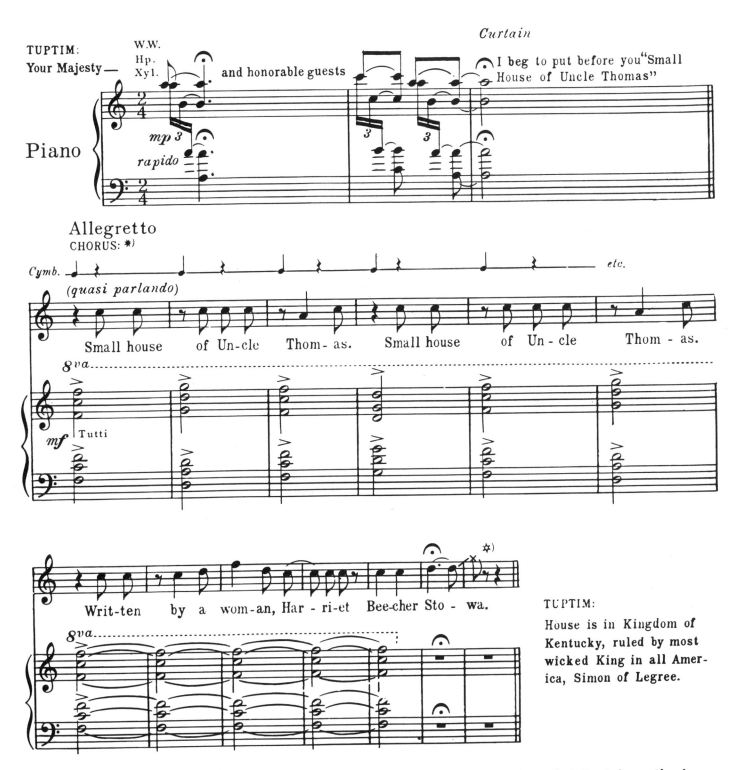

TUPTIM:

House is in Kingdom of Kentucky, ruled by most wicked King in all America, Simon of Legree.

✻) *The chorus, whenever speaking or singing in rhythm, beat Wood Blocks and Ancient Cymbals on the down beat. This applies to the entire ballet.*

✿) *Notes of this type: ✕ are spoken. An approximation of pitch is indicated throughout.*

Allegretto giocoso

Upstems to be played with felt on skin.
Downstems to be played with wood handle on rim (same stick).

(Loving friends dance a happy dance.)

TUPTIM:
Your Majesty, I beg to put before you one who is not happy, the slave Eliza.

4 Ben moderato e lamentoso

CHORUS:
Poor__ E - li - za, Poor__ E - li - za. Poor un-for-tu-nate sla - ve.

W.W.
Hns.
Hp.

TUPTIM:
Eliza's lord and master
King Simon of Legree.

She hates her lord and
master and fears him.

This King has sold her lover
to far away province of Oheeo

Stgs.

Gong on stage (with stick)

Gong on stage (with stick)

Lover's name is George.

TUPTIM:
Baby in her arms also called George.

TUPTIM:
Eliza say she run away,

CHORUS:
Ge-or - ge.

CHORUS:
Ge-or - ge.

The Journey

Simon Of Legree

*) Ad lib. wailing exclamations by different girls of the chorus.

TUPTIM: 12

Be - cause one slave has run a - way, Si-mon beat-ing ev -'ry slave.

TUPTIM:
Simon clever man.

He decide to hunt Eliza, not only with soldiers, but with scientific dogs who sniff and smell, and thereby discover all who run from King.

The Chase

*) *Throughout "Chase", in a steady cresc.*

Curtain in background opens, "Buddha" is seen sitting on a ladder in pose of meditation.

What will Bud - dha do?

ten.

TUPTIM:
Buddha make
a miracle!

Angel appears

Buddha send an Angel down. Angel make the wind blow cold.

W. W.
Hp.

Make the river water hard, hard enough to walk upon.

CHORUS: *(softly)*
Buddha make a miracle!

In tempo

Praise to Bud-dha!

The angel and Eliza shake hands solemnly

Gong on stage

Ice Skating Dance

TUPTIM:
Angel show her how to
walk on frozen water.

Molto calmo

Stgs. W.W.

con Ped.

TUPTIM:
Send from Heaven stars and blossoms.

Look like lace upon the sky.

Praise **to** **Bud - dha**

dim. molto

+ Hns.

TUPTIM:
So Eliza cross the river, hidden by this veil of lace.

morendo

Forgot to tell you name of
miracle: "Snow."

23 *Reentrance of Simon, guards and dogs. The snow flakes vanish. Eliza exits.*

Tempo di "Chase"

TUPTIM

Of a sud-den she can see Wick-ed Si-mon of Le-gree

W.W.

Cl.
Bsn *f* Trb.

Slid - ing cross the riv - er fast. With his blood - hounds and his slaves.

Molto marcato

Simon, guards and dogs dance grotesquely on ice

24

f Hns.
Stgs.
Trb.

Tutti

ff

sff

ff

W.W.
p Hp.
Stgs.

Angel appears holding the sun.

TUPTIM: What has happened to the river?

Budha has called out the sun.

simile
cresc. molto

Simon and slaves exit.

26 Tempo I⁰

TUPTIM:
On other side of river is pretty city, Canada, where Eliza sees lovely small

house. Guess who live in house?   *Uncle Thomas enters*

CHORUS:

Un - cle Thom - as.   Dear old Un - cle Thom - as.

* *This Vamp has to be played an indefinite number of times until the word cue: "live in house" comes up. This might take more or less bars than indicated here, since it depends on Tuptim's narration.*

Little Eva enters

TUPTIM:

CHORUS:

Little Topsy enters

.TUPTIM:

Lit - tle É - va. Bless - ed lit - tle E - va, Lit - tle Top - sy.

CHORUS:

Angel - George enters

TUPTIM:

Mis - chief mak - er, Top - sy. Lov - er George. Faith - ful lov - er,

TUPTIM:
Who is looking like angel to Eliza. They have all escaped from wicked Simon and make happy reunion.

Ge - or - ge.

W.W.
p Hp.

Happy Reunion Dance

Allegretto giocoso

27

Vns. Fl.
p

W.W.
Stgs.
mf

The whole ensemble enters

poco a poco

allargando molto

Tutti

Cymbal

+ Hns.
cresc.

Finale

28 **Slow March**

Tpt. & Cls.

Drum
on stage

ff Tutti

etc. throughout march

molto pesante

Cymbals

TUPTIM:
Topsy glad that Simon die,
Topsy dance for joy.

I tell you what Harriet Beecher Stowa say that Topsy say.

Tutti

I specks I'se de wickedest critter in de world!

But I do not believe Topsy is wicked critter. Because I too am glad for death of King. Of any King who pursues a slave who is unhappy and who wish to join her lover. And your Majesty, I wish to say to you - - - -

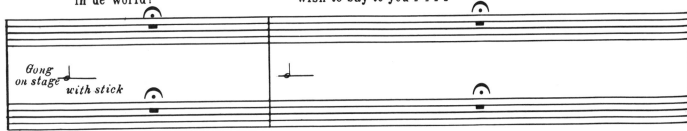

Gong
on stage with stick

W.W.
Hns.
Hp

Your Majesty and honorable guests!

I will tell you end of story.

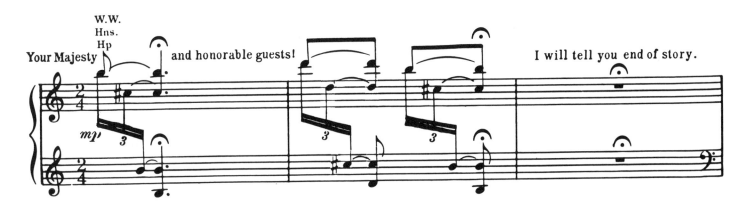

Is very sad ending. Buddha has saved Eliza. But with the blessings of Buddha also comes sacrifice.

Stgs.

Gong
on stage

Lento doloroso

CHORUS

Poor lit-tle E-va, Poor lit-tle E-va, Poor un-for-tu-nate child!

Stgs.
Hp.
W.W.
Hns.

TUPTIM: (speaking slowly)
Is Buddha's wish that Eva come to him and

Poor lit-tle E-va,

thank him personally for saving of Eliza and baby. And so she die and go to arms of Buddha.

Poor lit-tle E-va, Poor un-for-tu-nate child!

Curtain in background opens. "Buddha" stands on top of a ladder. Eva starts ascending to him while servants attach wings to her.

cresc. poco a poco

Tutti

Postlude Of Ballet

Incidental
(Change Of Scene)

Song Of The King

No. 38

Cue: KING: A silly complication of a pleasant simplicity.

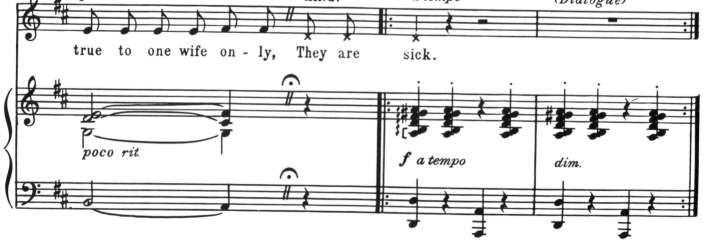

KING: *(spoken)* It is like old Siamese rhyme.

KING: *(sings)*

A girl must be like a blos-som with hon-ey for just one man. A man must live like hon-ey-bee and gath-er all he can. To fly from blos-som to blos-som, A hon-ey-bee must be free, But blos-som must not ev-er fly from bee, to bee, to bee.

No. 39

Shall We Dance?

Cue: A face... it speaks

Moderately (*brightly*) ♩ = 104

ANNA:

We've just been in-tro-duced, I do not know you well. But when the mu-sic start-ed, some-thing drew me to your side. So man-y men and girls Are in each oth-er's arms, It made me think we might be sim-i-lar-ly oc-cu-pied.

KING: *(spoken)*
Why do you stop? You dance pretty. Go on!

Go on! Go on! *(continue dialogue)*

KING: No, no, no, it is not right! (etc.)

KING:
They are not holding hands, like this.

KING: Was like this? No?   ANNA: Yes!   KING: Come!

lunga

molto rit

p Tutti

K *Anna and King dance Polka.*

ff very marked Polka rhythm

(*After applause*) KING:
Come, we do it again!

Encore

ff Tutti

Gong

sff

No. 40   Melos: My Lord And Master

Cue **TUPTIM:** Dead... Then I shall join him *(Tuptim screams)*

No. 41 # Processional

Prince enters.
Tempo I°

ff Tutti

Cue: INTERPRETER: Your highness, go no further!

Music stops on cue: INTERPRETER:
Your father is worse.

Exit: Cue: PRINCE: Go on with procession. *(Prince exits)*

No. 42 Reprise: Something Wonderful
(Letter Reading)

Cue: PRINCE: Please to read it to all of us.

Piano

Ending letter:
And much more difficult than generality!

ANNA: Come Louis!   *Anna exits.*   *(Curtain)*

Polka Doloroso

In front of Curtain.

Enter: Anna, Louis, Lady Thiang and Prince.

Very slowly

Lady Thiang and Prince exit.

LOUIS:
I thought you and the King were very angry with

each other.

LOUIS:
Was he as good a king as he could have been?

Tutti

No.44 Reprise: I Whistle A Happy Tune

rect And whis-tle a hap-py tune, So no one will sus-

pect I'm a - fraid._____ While shiv-er-ing in my

shoes, I strike a care-less pose And whis-tle a hap-py

tune And no one ev-er knows I'm a - fraid._____

3 *Dialogue.*

KING:
Whistle, you show them.

4

Anna whistles.

(Whistle)

No. 45

Finale Ultimo

Cue: ANNA: I hope so, your Majesty! I do hope so!

Molto moderato ♩ = 80   PRINCE: Up, rise up etc.

Piano

No. 46

Exit Music

Piano